Anna Bowles

Landscape with Mines

To Jen

Thanks for your support!

Anna

Landscape with Mines

published in the United Kingdom in 2025

by Mica Press & Campanula Books

https://micapress.uk | contact@micapress.uk

ISBN 978-1-869848-46-0

To the Ukrainians giving their lives for our freedom.

February the Thirty-Seventh

For Yulia

My Masters degree and I
knew Russia would never really invade.
Not *like this*.

★

In March, it's still February
as the map crackles and shrinks,
blackens towards Kyiv.

The reeling city bleeds people.
Your friends' kitchens yield mouldy onions,
champagne, washing-up and a refugee hamster.

Telegram pleads: *Driver needed…*
… elderly… medicine…
Empty playground. Train window.

On the hallway plastic mattress, sleepers
jostle out of rhythm with artillery
up in Irpin. You scream into a towel.

My gift from London:
Summary of official guidance
on how to survive a gas attack.

Your flatmate won't sleep near glass.
From the devil-glow of Irpin,
a shockwave rides south.

★

Each February dawn I levitate,
and feed myself sick on news.
Kyiv rocked overnight by new explosions.

Tanks crawl dogged round my brain.
It's, what, February the thirty-fifth?
Evacuation train doors slice off your family.

Fears that the capital will be encircled.
Kyiv is a thicket of hedgehogs, jilted kiosks
and posters for luxury flats in Bucha.

England's a pale concern of drifting phantoms.
I'm cracked on the London pavement, marvelling
at puddles of iridescent filth.

Sashko texts from a basement:
They are wiping Mariupol
from the face of the earth.

In Kyiv, the sirens give you three minutes' notice:
just enough time to boil coffee.
Your cat eyes the hamster.

★

Video call. *Occupied airstrike*
curfew missile checkpoint…
I hold a thimble to your haemorrhage,

then we voyage separately to dawn.
Time stamps in Telegram
show that you finally slept.

You say the night you first
dreamed of the war was
when it became real.

Translating Mariupol Diaries
March 2022

Sashko writes that to Mariupoltsi
corpses smell *ptomainic*... but I
wonder if we should render it as
the more familiar rotten *for Westerners?*
That gets shot down...
We shouldn't have to reduce our experience
to One Thousand Easiest English Words*!*
Corpses smell ~~rotten~~ *ptomainic.*

In 2021 they said,
I come from Mariupol.
In 2023, it's
After Mariupol.
Imagine it, a shift in your being
from *I live*
to *I did not die.* No,
it can't be translated
from body to sound...

Comments pop up in the Google Doc:
– *Thanks, I like how it reads in English.* –
– *:) Не за что. That's what I'm here for)))* –
I translate for friends.
Humans whose souls I thought
contiguous with mine
until they became
The Ukrainians.
What's *техническая вода* –
'technical' water? Oh, 'non-potable'.

I scope the original text,
slice an incision,
prise apart ribs,

grasp the meaning and
the shock the shock the shock
drubs through me,
second-hand screams
jam my throat
atrocity tears at synapse
until I cram it, seeping blood
into a rational package of English.

Her husband's corpse
in the shrapnelled living room
is too heavy to lift so Inna stays
and I go.
Listen
to Galochka. Listen
to Anya. Listen
to Veta. Listen
to throats crushed
under rubble.
I can't
reach so deep.
Some trace just got inside me
like sand in a laptop.

I never went to Mariupol…
I curl in my chair, my mind
crouching on Mariupol beach
playing idiom with shells
as the dustmeat city
crumbles at my back.
As dawn rises, I
release the screams:
white phosphorus gulls
over the Azov Sea.

The Photographer
April 2022

For Yulia

In a suburban park, the mass graves
are pegged with forensic bunting.
Bucha church strains upward
as stewards heft the raw-backed clay.

De-miners signal the all-clear, and hell's
car-park attendants marshal the journalists
in orderly babel. The world laments
through French, Japanese and default English.

Beyond the cordon, binbags flap
and dew-sluiced relicts beckon.
The camera swings from your neck
and mud spittles your cheeks

as you crouch to log each atrocity.
It's worse every time it's the same.

Finally you cap your lens, start the car
and jolt back down the pillaged street.
The rear-view mirror is ghosts.
The shattered windows are ghosts.

At home, you drop 90GB to the newsroom;
watch corpses metastasize on Twitter.

There is no god. There is your precision.

Lviv in Wartime
March 2023

Elegant, these western cities.
The war is mostly inferred.
When the sirens sound, folk hide –
it's serious, but statistically not fatal.

Families from Kherson cram the hostels
or sub-let from locals who fled to Poland,
putting down scrawny and tentative roots,
just firm enough not to blow over the border.

In Lviv, soldiers amble with sweethearts,
veterans lilt down Uzhhorod alleys,
and volunteers weave camouflage nets
or dry rations for soldiers out east.

On the outermost nerve of collective
endurance, folk nurse a savourless calm,
visit the park, the castle, museums,
the aquarium where the catfish circle,

chafing their whiskers to pustulent nubs.
What cannot be spoken lies sleepless
in Uzhhorod. What cannot be borne
sets down in Lviv to suffer its days.

Night Train to Zaporizhzhia

March 2023

Two bunks spare in our four-person coupe.
Midnight halt: a rifle butt pokes through the door.

Grandmother Olga – she was lonely in Slovakia,
so let Putin do his worst, she's coming home –

near-levitates in opprobrium. Butt retreats…
till his officer snaps, *You sleep there or in the corridor!*

He shuffles in. Olga glares poison – in her head it's 2014,
when the army was all drunks and hoodlums –

while I smile my foreigner smile, excusing myself
an opinion as Butt's mate springs over my head

and Butt, above Olga, fashions his bunk
as a fortress of kit bags. Finally we sleep.

Morning: the sink's broken. Butt uses a half-can
of body spray conquering his pit-pong

and then settles by Olga who shows him
her family photos. A nice lad, is Rifle,

I see her decide as she stabs an invisible
mid-air Europe, grumbling: *Children up here,*

friends over there, me stuck down here,
it's too much, it really is.

She cradles his phone:
pictures of his baby daughter.

Rifle's mate never speaks.
Crewcut. Haunted look. Beware.

Landscape with Mines
Kharkiv oblast, March 2023

In Kharkiv, the fields have teeth.
The roadside trenches clutch darkness

as volunteers bringing tools to the village
drive slowly past the fluttering markers.

The flaking snout of the burnt-out tank
directs us better than satnav.

★

Stay on the path.
We thread from the crater on the road
to the crater in Natalia's yard.

*Six months on the front line, we
changed hands how many times?*
She mimes a helicopter strafing.

A white puff in the distance!
Don't worry, it's just sappers.

The funeral was yesterday.
The land's heave of grief

and its terrible patience. Trees
brandish mistletoe fists at the sky.

★

Leaving, we watch a controlled burn.
The flames snuffle, low and unhurried,

perhaps clear to the border, where
barbed wire sutures past to future.

Westward, through fields stippled with wheat,
Sashko whispers: *Ukraine is alive.*

The setting sun dimples the earth;
the sky makes truce.

Consider forgiveness. The Russians lay mines
shaped like toys, like petals, like butterflies.

Grandmother Rising
Zaporizhzhia, April 2023

Lyudmila greets the volunteers
bringing cancer meds. Offers tea.
Oh, no need to get up.

Nevertheless, she hefts from the armrests;
slips back. *Give me a moment.*
We hover, respectful, although

we don't fancy her chances.
But Lyudmila saw off Hitler
and Stalin. She rises now,

steadies herself on a ready arm.
A moment, my dears.
She sways as she grasps

an unseen moment. Then lopes
into the kitchen to pour us tea.
Fresh withered leaves and sweet lemon.

The news says the war is at stalemate.
We drink the will that binds us, as to
the east Lyudmila's son raises a rifle.

Tania's House
Kherson oblast, September 2023

Tania's house will not leave her.
Her headscarf blooms as she potters
around the garden, checking for mines.

The Russians razed the village, home by home
by home by home by home and filmed it.
Tania mixes mortar in the dead pig's bucket.

The roof sags tenderly over her, as she scours
the kitchen rubble. Artillery still booms
at night, as stars drip into the bath.

The tabby mouser survived. And the tray
with the daisies. Her best pan, too,
only holed through one side. Tania

wields patience; veined meticulous
hands rekindling the dented stove.
Catch aid workers down here!

The days will shorten and winter grasp,
and no one forgets the death they didn't
die, no matter how hard they prayed.

White creases flex on Tania's weathered neck
as she bends, mixing mortar in that old bucket,
preparing the house. For her son will return.

Art Therapy at Hostel No. 14
Kharkiv, August 2023

They open the playroom once a week
if enough volunteers come.

Seven-year-old Vasyl follows me round
waving Google Translate: ***We go outside?***

I explain that I speak his language.
I enunciate clearly, *Not today. It's art.*

His gaze wanders the shelves
of unopened 1,000-piece jigsaws…

ten seconds later the phone's back
under my nose: ***We eat pizza?***

No. Sit down quietly and draw like Katia.
I do the rounds. Ten new faces today,

there was mandatory evacuation from—
We go to movies?

He doesn't *look* traumatised
though maybe that's like saying

you can't see water when you're drowning—
We go to movies?

No. Though maybe we should do pizza again,
good pics for the foreign donors… ***We go to theme park?***

Christ. The cinemas are boarded up.
The theme park's bombed out.

Katia's drawing a missile strike. Orange entrails.
Vasyl sits, finally, stealing her crayon.

Soon he'll ask,
We go home?

in ukrainian kitchens
autumn 2023

in kyiv an off-white bakelite radio
spews news from every front.
there's a vial of azov sea on the shelf.
a fundraising mascot with painted eyes.
… driving back to the medical point,
she skidded on the weir…

hi, veta, tea?
she's on leave from training.
what's everyone up to?
i was going to volunteer with…
… but near bakhmut they
anti-tank missile
               shrug
          yeah, read about that
need another plan, then

artists boil humanitarian pasta.
in mariupol, galochka cupped snails,
slipped them safe from the road to the grass.
my friend in st petersburg is so afraid,
her son, i'd rather be here…

in this borrowed kyiv kitchen
she massages her temples.
we can't become as bad
as them, we just can't…

mm, how would we do that?
               i mean, how would we *do* that?

               yuri drove over corpses.
        bump   bump   bump   bump

so veta says
i want to kill russians i want to kill
enemies of donbas.
she was bombed out in avdiivka, in mariupol,
bombed
till her soul blazes with love
to extinguish this   perversion
in her own blood, the friend *raped and tortured,*
boyfriend killed himself, gave the baby to…

… message from b. in kharkiv: *sorry,*
can't talk tonight, gotta sit
          with my buddy, his mate was…

… in a summer kitchen in kryvyi rih
there's warm light, succulent melons.
these days, the crickets imitate the sirens.
in zaporizhzhia we buy too much wine,
so anna says *we're stocked up for if*
the nuclear power station blows,
then sashko's like, *never mind fallout,*
it's less destructive than rockets
laughter
                    laughter

                                        laughter

          …

everyone has started to look like the war,
everywhere the darkness
is hunting. crashing
the windows nightly,
the shrapnel
routine now
in every love.

on the 114 bus to podil, think. of. nothing.

… death in a whatsapp bubble –

commander had a list: Oleh Lypka, Dmytro Kovalchuk, Maryna Tsaran, Danylo Filonenko, Oleksandr Kravets, Viktor Tkachenko, Danylo Hryb, Iryna Kvasha, Ihor Hevko, Serhii Bondar, Ivan Boyko…

no, it's fine, we keep going.

believe. we have learned

how to divide life by zero.

Aid Drop
Donetsk oblast, October 2024

Just down the road from the bombed-out ostrich farm,
an armoured car skulks beneath a half-shattered tree.

We're watching for drones, awaiting the all-clear
to proceed to the village hall, which is mostly standing.

The woman's blouse is a turbid pink as she stomps
towards us – no, at us – eyes weirdly unseeing…

I concede her point: groceries delivered by armoured car,
it's so rancorously absurd, the world must be glitching.

From a half-smashed blue door, is that a child's cry?
No. The shelling's getting nearer. And so is she.

The radio: *Clear to proceed.* The woman swerves
to trudge round us, eyes dead with purpose – oh,

come back! We'll evacuate you, mother! To
the harassed daughter, the overcrowded hostel…

As well ask the tree to run from its roots, the rubble
to phone its children. Hope is no longer of interest.

Vigil

Donetsk oblast, October 2024

The last cigarette of the day. In the quiet yard
a blanket around his shoulders, his arm around her.

The eastern front glimmers and belches.
A stray cat huddles by the front door. Don't

let it in, it'll never leave.

The blanket is slipping from his back to hers.
Some poor sod in Pokrovsk got their jaw blown off.

He says, *We may have to evacuate. Before the front
collapses. Before the artillery reaches Kramatorsk.*

His fingers trace her shrapnel scars. The stars
glimmer with unreachable contempt. She says,

*I haven't given up, but let me
be terrified. Just for a while,
let me be terrified.*

We Are Not in This Field
Winter 2024

We are not in this field. We are humanitarians,
headed to the village with thermal underwear
in boxes stamped *Civilian Use Only.*

The daylight is fading. Freezing rain.
The soldier says there were ninety in his battalion,
forty are left… But we are not in this field.

My fists are jammed hard into my pockets.
The livestock are gone. The villagers said,
Don't waste stuff on us, the army need it.

The soldier backs his van up to ours. We might
mislay a box or two, or forget some paperwork.
As humanitarians, we were not in this field.

In a month, the village will be rubble. The Russians
will rape the women in this field. The soldier's eyes gleam.
As he tells us about his kids, he is not in this field.

Author's Note

I did not expect to find myself in this field. Here I am, though, sitting in a rented flat in Kramatorsk, less than 20 km from the front line in a European war, listening to explosions in the city and watching notifications about spy drones popping up in the local Telegram news channel. Russia is trying to cut the supply lines. The West is alternately wringing its hands and pretending this isn't happening or that we can do nothing to stop it.

Since the full-scale invasion in February 2022, I've spent about a year in Ukraine over the course of six trips. During that time I've volunteered in various ways, some of which are documented in this collection. I began to write poetry three days after the invasion, as a way of processing my feelings, and it's grown into a means of bearing witness. Literature responds more slowly to events than a blog does, but also more deeply. I hope this pamphlet provides a glimpse of war and some insight into why and how it is relevant to those physically far away.

By the time you read this, perhaps some kind of peace agreement will have been signed between Ukraine and Russia. Perhaps war poems will become historical curios. Perhaps Russia's colonial mindset will evaporate without the West needing to confront it. Or perhaps not.

We are all in this field.

Anna Bowles, Kramatorsk, Ukraine, 24 September 2025

My travel blog can be found at annabowles.substack.com.

Acknowledgements

My thanks to the editors and judges of the following journals and competitions in which some of these poems have previously appeared:

'February the Thirty-Seventh' commended in the Poetry Wales Competition 2025
'Translating Mariupol Diaries' first published in *Magma* 92
'The Photographer' first published in *Poetry Salzburg* 42
'Lviv in Wartime' first published in *Pennine Platform* 97
'Night Train to Zaporizhzhia' first published in *Pennine Platform* 97
'Landscape with Mines' first published in *Magma* 90
'Grandmother Rising' first published in *The Four-Faced Liar* 3
'Tania's House' awarded second prize in the Edward Thomas Fellowship competition 2025
'Art Therapy at Hostel No. 14' awarded third prize in the Wolverhampton Literature Festival Competition 2025
'in ukrainian kitchens' first published in *Magma* 90
'Aid Drop' awarded second prize in the Ironbridge Festival Poetry Competition 2025
'Vigil' commended in the South Downs Poetry Prize 2025
'We Are Not in This Field' first published in *Collateral Journal* 9.3

My huge thanks to Les Bell for pulling *Landscape with Mines* out of his submission pile and not only publishing it, but choosing to do so on an expedited schedule because of the importance of the subject matter. I feel honoured by this level of commitment to my work. To Mariia Pronina for designing the wonderful cover, and for giving me the chance to work with her at Ptichka Fund to retrieve teenagers from Russia and occupied territory. To Sashko Protyah and Yulia Serdyukova, and many hundreds of other local and sometimes foreign volunteers who I've met, worked with and interviewed during my time in Ukraine; and also to Yulia for her long-term support of my writing.

To Judy Brown for her editorial insight and generosity with her time, and Katrina Naomi for her suggestions on my early batches of poems. Though before anyone else there was Ros Taylor, who looked at the first poems I'd written in thirty years, a few days after the full-scale invasion, and then helped me orient myself as a poet.

And finally to my beloved husband Philip, whose total, and totally honest, incomprehension of poetry, combined with unwavering support, brings joy to my heart.

Ukrainian Poetry

If you've enjoyed this pamphlet, please do investigate the work of contemporary Ukrainian poets, who are increasingly being translated into English. Writing is for them is not just an important means of expression, but an act of resistance and a statement of survival. Here are a few recommendations:

Artur Dron: *We Were Here*
Halyna Kruk: *A Crash Course in Molotov Cocktails*
Oksana Maksymchuk: *Still City: a Diary of an Invasion*
Serhiy Zhadan: *How Fire Descends: New and Selected Poems*

Cover Artist

Mariia Pronina was displaced from her hometown of Donetsk and her adopted city of Mariupol, and now lives in Kyiv, where she continues her work with collage. The six elements of the sky are taken from the six regions of Ukraine that are currently occupied, have been deoccupied or are the scenes of active fighting, while the forest and flowers come from the border between Kharkiv and Donetsk regions. The mines, weapons and broken toys are taken from media coverage of the attacks on Ukraine, and public safety information booklets. Mariia is available for commissions and can be contacted at mpronina14@ukr.net.

www.ingramcontent.com/pod-product-compliance
Ingram Content Group UK Ltd.
Pitfield, Milton Keynes, MK11 3LW, UK
UKHW050453170126
466997UK00008B/31